S0-BFA-287

GREEN BERET CHAPLAIN

FR. MIKE ORTIZ

Copyright © 2013 by Fr. Mike Ortiz.

Library of Congress Control Number:		2013915947
ISBN:	Hardcover	978-1-4836-9366-8
	Softcover	978-1-4836-9365-1
	Ebook	978-1-4836-9367-5

All rights reserved. No part of this book may be reproduced or transmitted in any form or by any means, electronic or mechanical, including photocopying, recording, or by any information storage and retrieval system, without permission in writing from the copyright owner.

This book was printed in the United States of America.

Rev. date: 09/16/2013

To order additional copies of this book, contact:
Xlibris LLC
1-888-795-4274
www.Xlibris.com
Orders@Xlibris.com
139950

CONTENTS

DEDICATION

THIS BOOK IS DEDICATED TO THE
THE CHAPLAINS OF ALL BRANCHES OF THE
MILITARY SERVICES
AND ALL MEMBERS OF THE
"GREEN BERETS"

VOLUNTEERING
1965

It was late fall, 1965 and I sat just outside the doctor's office, my nervous hand holding a glass of water and a pounding heart uttering a silent prayer. I felt as I imagine a young husband must feel as he waits to hear that his wife has just delivered their first baby. The doctor had seen the disappointing look on my face after he told me that my back surgery was a problem and so he told me to sit and wait while he made a call. After what seemed like an eternity he came out, suddenly put out his hand and with a smile and said: "Congratulations, Reverend, I've just gotten off the phone with the Chief of Surgeons Office and they have given you a medical waiver." I was tempted to give him a big bear hug, this doctor in an Army uniform, but only shook his hand, looked up to heaven, whispering: "Thank you Jesus".

This was my third and final attempt to be a chaplain in the Armed Forces. The first was while I was stationed in a mission church and school in northern Mississippi. I had finally, after years of begging, received permission from my Religious Superior, and the Catholic Endorsing Agency to volunteer for the chaplaincy. As a kid I often dreamed of becoming a Marine and now it seemed a reality; so I drove to the nearest Navy Recruiting Station in Nashville, Tennessee. In filling out the questionnaire (the same for all the branches) I stated that about nine years previously I had back surgery (laminectomy). I was now thirty-seven years old but in good physical condition. The young sailor behind the desk quickly told me that I was medically disqualified, no ifs, ands or buts. I returned to my mission in Holly Springs, and decided to try the Air Force, after all, their chaplains operated very much like civilian ministers. In this second attempt I decided to write a personal letter to the Air Force Chief of Chaplain, Major General Chess, and a Roman Catholic Priest. Again I received the same response. "The life of a chaplain in our Air Force is very tough, physically and mentally. We are sorry, but we cannot accept you." I had told him that, in spite of age and an old surgery, I would be willing to fly to San Antonio and take any physical testing to prove I was fit. "Regulations are regulations," he said. What a letdown!

I had not planned to join the Army chaplaincy, but it was now the only branch available. I expressed my frustration to a priest friend of mine who had served as a chaplain for the Navy and then the Army. He was now retired and living in Milwaukee, Wisconsin and invited me to fly up to Milwaukee and try the Army Recruiting Station there.

Important to note is that the Army surgeon told me the same news about my being disqualified. The big difference was that he showed some compassion and did what the other branches could have done. He spoke on my behalf and convinced the Chief of Surgeons that I was physically fit and able to perform my duties as a chaplain. I'm convinced that the Good Lord was influential in all this. As I mentioned before, I had really not considered the Army. It seemed too conventional for me, too huge; but in completing the required forms at the Recruiting Station one of the questions asked was to what type of unit I would like to be assigned. There was Infantry, Armor, Airborne, Aviation, Signal, Medical, etc. None seemed all that appealing to me. Then, I vaguely remembered reading about a relatively new unit; senior enlisted and officers called Special Forces.

Officially approved in 1952, they were considered the elite unit of all the branches of the military. Made up of mostly older NCOs (non-commissioned officers), I was intrigued by the make-up of their units. The "A Team" was a unit of two officers and ten sergeants. Each team had two heavy weapons experts, two light weapons experts, two communications experts. Most learned to speak a foreign language and all were experts in conducting unconventional type warfare. Once qualified, they wore a Green Beret. Robin Moore brought these men into the spotlight with his song: The Ballet of the Green Beret: "One hundred men will test today, but only three win the Green Beret". Well . . . , since neither the Navy nor the Air Force would accept me, I would prove to them, and anyone else, that I would be qualified with the "best of the best". I wrote down on that form: "Special Forces". I hoped and prayed that I would be accepted.

FORT HAMILTON, NEW YORK
1966

Before flying to New York, I was sworn in as a First Lieutenant and began buying my uniforms, shoes, and etcetera. During this exciting time I reflected on what my past had been as a Parish Priest and what it would be like as a Military Chaplain. I would be leaving relatives, friends, students I had learned to love so much. I would be separating myself from the religious community to which I had been attached for so long.

The transition from civilian Priest to military Chaplain would be difficult but I was determined mentally, spiritually, and physically to reach that goal.

Arriving at Fort Hamilton, I was with almost one hundred ministers of different approved denominations, Rabbis, and Catholic Priests, and most of us "newbies". Fort Hamilton was a small Army Installation located on the Brooklyn side of the Verazzano Bridge. Each chaplain had his own room, completely furnished. We all quickly learned what a PX (Post Exchange) and Commissary (Grocery Store) meant. We were introduced to the faculty, and all personnel involved in our Basic Training. One of my classmates was a Lutheran Minister by the name of John Zilvazy. He became a close friend once we found out we were from the same home town in Indiana and because he had had prior service as an enlisted man. With his help I learned how to ready my uniforms, where to pin on my Lieutenant bars, the chaplain's crest, my name tag, the Special Forces shoulder patch, and the proper wearing of that beautiful "Green Beret."

The class was composed of ministers of varied approved religious denominations and we called ourselves the "Brotherhood of Ministers". We learned to work together, help each other, and pray together. Ecumenism at its best. We began each day with PT (physical training) quick shower and breakfast and on to classroom work. Experienced we might be in ministerial work, we were taught how to deal with young men and women involved in combat, the wounded, the dying, those suffering traumatic distress.

Our weekends were usually free so many would take the subway to the "Big Apple", take in a Broadway play or movie, see the sights, or just relax after a hard week of classroom work. Some classmates would volunteer their time in the neighboring churches. One day another of my Protestant classmates asked if I would be willing to go aboard a Navy Carrier with him and celebrate a Mass for the Catholic sailors aboard. They had no Priest and they couldn't leave ship. I went with the Chaplain but kept saying to myself: "Aha! Now, the Navy will accept me as an Army Chaplain and wearing a Green Beret!"

The Army's regimental crest is a beautiful symbol of what we are all about. It is an infantry blue shield on top of which is a golden wreath surrounding a shepherd's crook and the numbers 1775. These represented the Chaplain's pastoral ministry and the year it was founded. The open book and the dove with olive branch in its beak represent the Chaplain's mission to deter war and strive for peace. The motto beneath the shield, Pro Deo et Patria, translates: For God and Country.

Upon completion of our classroom work the class was then moved to Fort Dix, New Jersey, where we were to bivouac for a week, and, what a week! We lived in tents, prepared our own MREs (meals ready to eat), slushed through muddy paths, learned to fire weapons (the only weapon I had ever fired was a Red Ryder BB rifle), toss live grenades, don a gas mask and spend time in a gas chamber, crawl under barbed wire while having a machine gun fired over our heads, read a map eat those MREs. I thought that recreational camping was rough! We were all one happy group of candidates when we returned to the luxury of Fort Hamilton.

THIRD SPECIAL FORCES GROUP
FORT BRAGG, NORTH CAROLINA
1966-1967

After graduation we all had our orders, some for overseas, most to an installation in CONUS (Continental United States). Two other chaplains and I headed to Ft. Bragg, home of the Infantry, Officer Candidate School and headquarters for the Third SFG. It is a sprawling, busy military base located adjacent to the city of Fayetteville. Typical of any town or city near a military installation, it abounds in motels, night clubs, restaurants, massage parlors, etc. Upon my arrival I was met and welcomed by the Senior Chaplain, a wonderful, helpful Protestant man who became a good mentor. He escorted me to headquarters where I was greeted very enthusiastically, but immediately placed on orders to go through Airborne training at Fort Benning, Georgia.

Things were moving fast, so I began increasing my daily PT. My Senior Chaplain introduced me to every office and training area. At this particular time the Third Special Forces Group had been given the special mission of training about 400 new recruits, fresh from civilian life. One of my tasks was to give the monthly "Character Guidance" class to these "young kids". I was as nervous as they were the first time I got up on the theatre stage, but not before doing a "dry run" that is, give my presentation to an empty theatre with only he being present.

In my spare time, before reporting to the Airborne school, I tried to learn as much as I could about Special Forces. First of all, I learned that the men were professional; in fact they preferred to be known as the "Quiet Professionals". Only mature, physically fit, airborne type sergeants, officers, and graduates of the special Q" (qualification) course, would be accepted. I wasn't yet qualified, not yet airborne, but I believe, physically fit, and determined to fulfill all requirements, even be a qualified HALO and SCUBA chaplain. I wanted that "Green Beret"! I loved the idea that they were unconventional. They were trained to "infiltrate", to work for and with the people struggling for a democracy; their motto "De Oppresso Liber", (Liberator of the Oppressed) meant a lot to me. When I would read about the work they were doing in Vietnam: training the indigenous, building clinics, schools, digging wells for water, utilizing their medical knowledge in caring for the sick. I wanted to be a part of that group of soldiers. In those early years there were five active Groups: the 1st Group on Okinawa, the 3rd Group at Fort Bragg, NC, the 5th Group in Vietnam, the 8th Group in Panama, and the 10th in Germany.

Each Group was made up of three battalions with three companies each and each company had six "A" teams consisting of twelve men. I learned that back in 1952 President John F. Kennedy, a Navy veteran, had been briefed about this special unit called the 10th Special Forces Group and the unconventional way in which they operated, and the funny European style headgear they unofficially wore. He planned an official visit to the 82nd Airborne Division located at Ft. Bragg so he sent down word that he also planned to visit this group of professionals and that they were authorized to wear that "Green Beret". In fact, I recall his words about that beret: "a symbol of excellence, a badge of courage, a mark of distinction, the fight for freedom."

AIRBORNE SCHOOL
FORT BENNING, GEORGIA
1967

It wasn't long after my assignment to Fort Bragg that I received orders for the Home of the Airborne. John Silvazy, the Protestant chaplain from my home town, and I drove down to Fort Benning. We were definitely older than the hundreds of young soldiers undergoing the same training we would be involved in. Were we up to it? Three weeks of tough PT and constant harassment of those tough-looking NCO (non-commissioned officer) instructors we called: "Black Hats"? I worried a bit.

Columbus, Georgia is definitely an "airborne" city. Stores, bars, military stores, motels, massage parlors, laundromats, restaurants, etc., cater to the hundreds of students that come here to become paratroopers.

We all were housed in old World War II barracks. They were so sparse I was reminded of the "cell" I lived in while going through "boot camp" with the religious community to which I belonged. The bunk beds were just a few feet from each other, with a wooden Army trunk at the foot of each bunk. We all have heard tales about the sergeant dropping a coin on a newly made bunk which had to bounce when dropped, or the fatigues being starched, or the boots being "spit-shined", or the soldier having an "Airborne hair-cut". Well, believe me, it's all very true. I would spend most of my evenings getting my uniform ready and "spit-shining" those muddy boots. Woe to any student, officer or enlisted, if he failed the early morning inspection. Students for the Airborne course came from all branches of the service, Army, Navy, Air Force, and Marines. The competition was unbelievable.

Columbus, like Fayetteville, was a "military city". It offered everything for the students' pleasure. The instructors were all sergeants and master jumpers. There was a professionalism in all they did and there was a no nonsense attitude about their instructions. Among these instructors, were two young but experienced females that just amazed all the students. One of the male instructors seemed to "zero in on me" from the very first day. He was a short, stocky southern man with an unlit stub of a cigar in his mouth. With a deep drawl he would stare steel green beady eyes, unlit cigar between his teeth and shout: "Chaplain, Ah don't think y'all are gonna make it! . . . Are you?" I would shout back: "Yes, Sergeant Airborne. I'm gonna make it!" All of a sudden he would yell, "Drop! Drop!" meaning I was to drop to the ground and do twenty to thirty push-ups, and shout: "Airborne, Sergeant". I felt that he was always looking for me during our short breaks so I would try to hide behind the water tank or go to the latrine. He would always find me. It was only on graduation day that he had a huge smile on his face and pinned the silver wings on my chest.

The three week course was broken down into Ground Week: with PT and a three mile run, learning the basics of exiting out of a plane, and exiting out of a thirty-four foot tower: Tower week, increased runs, learning how to control our descent with "risers", and pulled up to a steel 250 foot tower and released with free-falling parachute: Jump week, actually making five real jumps out of a C-119, a C-130, or a C-5. On my fourth night jump I didn't make a proper parachute landing fall (PLF), so I injured my right leg. Returning to my bunk I rubbed a whole tube of Ben Gay on my thigh and dared not report to the medics because I knew I would be dropped from the class and start the course all over again. So, early the next morning I wrapped a pillow around the leg, tucked it under my trousers, and limped to the airfield determined to finish. One of the Black Hats watched me and was about to pull me out of line until I persuaded him that I was fine.

Flying toward the DZ (drop zone), crammed into a plane so tight with a twenty-nine pound parachute on your back, reserve chute snapped to your chest, jumping out of a perfectly good airplane . . . . I wondered why was I doing this? Well, back in 1475 Leonardo da Vinci had proven that it was possible.

The Russians had used parachutes to drop their infantry into battle. In 1939 our Army had 47 volunteers parachute right on to these very drop zones. So, what the heck! We were jumping from around 1,200 feet and it would take about 8.8 seconds for my chute open. I prayed: "Help me Lord!" Suddenly I hear the Jumpmaster shout: "Ten minutes", and we all jump up from our seats, and hook our static line to the plane's overhead cable. A red light on the open door suddenly turns green and the Jumpmaster gives the command to shuffle to the door.

"GO"! He yelled above the noise and out we go! What an experience! My eyes were shut tight the first few seconds but quickly opened to see whether my canopy had opened and I got a glimpse of those beautiful skies and that lovely ground I would land on.

To this day, some thirty six years after I earned those jump wings, I still get all excited just thinking about jump school and the rigid discipline during training but most of all the thrill of floating down to earth.

FIRST SPECIAL FORCES
OKINAWA, JAPAN
1967-1968

During jump week I received a call from the Special Forces Chaplain at JFK Center in Fort Bragg, Fr. Waldie, informing me that I had received overseas orders assigning me to the First Special Forces Group on Okinawa. Though I thought it was a bit soon, since I had just begun to learn more about Special Forces. I nevertheless was overjoyed to learn that I would continue to wear that Green Beret. I had planned to go through the "Q" (Qualification) Course at Camp McCall and earn the full flash for my beret, but I knew that I could earn my "Prefix 3" at a later date. I took a thirty day leave in Indiana and then flew Space A (space available) to San Francisco where I met up with a veteran who was returning to Vietnam for a second tour. In those days we still wore our uniforms whenever we went downtown so we both decided to have dinner together at some restaurant in down town San Francisco. I was surprised when a group of hippies came up to us, shouting obscenities and spitting at us, but my friend took it all in stride. He had been through this before.

I landed at Kadena Air Force Base in Okinawa on a hot humid day. It was my first overseas assignment, so I reported to the Group's headquarters. The commander, a Colonel Ladd, and senior Chaplain Dick Combs, did everything to make me feel at home.

I would soon find out that this assignment was ideal for me because I would get all the necessary training for my future mission in Vietnam.

Okinawa is known by Americans because of the heroic battle and victory by our Marines. It is an island only about fourteen miles in width and some seventy miles in length made up mostly of volcanic rock. It is hot and humid in the summer visited by very strong hurricanes. The Air Force had an Air Base with well manicured lawns, golf course, and Officer's Club. The Navy had a base to which our supply ships docked to load and unload what the American servicemen and dependents needed. The Army had a huge logistics base adjacent to the Navy's Port, a Communications unit and a fairly large Hospital. The 3rd Special Forces Group had a number of locations where specialized training was given to the Green Berets who would go TDY (temporary duty), or a permanent assignment to the 5th Special Group in Vietnam.

Our chaplain offices were in a quonset hut near the Army's hospital. The BOQ (bachelor officer quarters) buildings were a two family type sections with bedroom and bathroom for each and a common kitchen and living room. Mine was very close to the Officer's Club so I ate most of my meals there. More often I would drive up to the Navy's Club where the meals were much better. The Army, Navy, Air Force, and Marines were well established since the Island was closest to Japan. We Catholic Chaplains from all the Services would get together at least once a month and spend a day in prayer at an American missionary's home. I came to appreciate the times we had together for spiritual reflection. Once a year we would fly to Japan for a week's spiritual retreat at Kyoto's Maryknoll retreat center. I soon realized that the assignment to this Group was for me the best. The 3rd SFG's primary mission was to train and prepare A Teams. This being the case, HALO and SCUBA courses were offered. A kind of "gentleman's Q Course" could qualify the individuals, like me, to "go for it". Some of the training would take place in Laos, Lopburi Thailand, Korea, and Japan. In no other Group would I have had the opportunities that were offered here on this small Island. Actually, my men would challenge me; almost dare me, to qualify. I was out to prove that I was able to compete and become qualified. For example, although I had enjoyed swimming on Lake Michigan as a teenager, I wasn't too sure I would enjoy swimming in shark infested waters. The SCUBA team told me they needed a chaplain to dive down with their students and give the benediction on graduation day. How on earth could I say a prayer and benediction with my gear and the mask? And what about the sharks?

They just laughed and told me not to worry. I could just give a signal to the graduates for a moment of silent prayer. As for the sharks? They probably would pause for a moment of silence also.

The HALO (high altitude low opening) instructors also challenged me. "Not to worry", they would say, "You will be so close to your maker that He will make sure you open that chute on time and that your oxygen tank is working properly." I do remember the very first jump I made from about 10,000 feet. How beautiful the clouds, how silent the surroundings, but how tiny that island of Okinawa seemed to be.

The trek through the jungle in the island was an event that taught me to rely on buddies. A handful of us started out one evening, with an experienced NCO and a rucksack full of what we would use or need. Here I was now, a thirty-eight year old chaplain, trudging along with a much, much younger group of soldiers.

Toward the end of the exercise I was really beat and didn't believe I could continue. A young doctor, also going through the exercise pulls me over and hands me a green capsule he called an "upper" and tells me to take it with some water. You won't believe this, but I was so energized that I shot up to the head of the group. Again I imagined God telling me: "Go for it"! There were so many other opportunities for training and preparing for an assignment which I knew would come. Time was passing by so quickly.

I accompanied a team flying to Seoul, Korea once. We were to jump on to the river bank with full gear and "Alice". An Alice is an extra pack, or bundle, which the jumper attaches to his chute with a "tether", or cord. A few hundred feet before landing, the jumper releases the Alice but is still attached to the harness of the jumper. I suppose that I had not properly attached that tether, so I lost it in the soggy river bank and couldn't find it even with the help of some buddies. I was never to live this incident down.

I managed to go on many TDY (temporary duty) trips with teams, to exotic places like Bangkok, Thailand and Cambodia. I even got an R&R (rest and recreation) and went to Sydney, Australia, and Taiwan. So many people have the mistaken belief that Special Forces soldiers don't have and don't want Chaplains. I know from experience that these hard charging men are most appreciative of having their own chaplain. Once, while making a HALO jump I injured my back, had surgery, and was convalescing in the Camp Kue Army Hospital, when in comes one of my sergeants with John Wayne, "The Duke", to visit me in my hospital room. The movie star, whom I thought of as my idol, was "massive". He reaches out his huge hand and asks how I was doing. All I could mutter was: "I'm fine, Mr. Duke". John Wayne had come to Okinawa in search of a location for his film; The Green Berets.

Another proof was when the senior Catholic Chaplain, Ralph Murray, attempted to get me transferred permanently to the large Army hospital on the Island. Here I was just a lowly First Lieutenant and telling a Colonel that he couldn't do that because I had specific orders assigning me to Special Forces. When my commander heard of this, and he was the one responsible for cutting the orders, he had orders cut keeping me in the Special Forces Group but with additional duty to the hospital. Father Murray and the hospital commander were never friendly with me after that, but my commander had said: "We are not about to lose you".

I continued with my work and would spend half the day working at the hospital and with my Special Forces Group.

In addition to these duties I also covered a covert signal unit in the Southern part of the Island as well as (would you believe?) the Marines at their Camp Hansen. I was reaching the end of my tour on Okinawa and hoping for an assignment with another Special Forces Group. I didn't dare inform the Chief of Chaplain's Office about my back surgery for fear I would be assigned to a "leg" unit.

FORT BENNING, GEORGIA
1967-1968

To my surprise I received orders to the Jump School at Fort Benning, Georgia. Protestant Chaplain Roman and I would jump with each class at least once during their jump week. Our battalion commander was a little man who once approached me to tell me that his Protestant chaplain spent more time with the students than I did. I reminded him that I had to also cover OCS (Officer Candidate School) as well the Rangers. He warned me that he was my rater and I had better spend more time with his troops. I went to the Brigade commander who quickly straightened him out.

This was to occur on various assignments because some commanders didn't understand that Catholic Chaplains covered more units than others due to an overall shortage of Catholic Priests.

FIFTH SPECIAL FORCES GROUP
VIETNAM
1968-1969

After a short leave I flew to Hawaii and then on to DaNang, Vietnam. Since I had specific orders I felt I should get a flight to Nha Trang, where the Group's headquarters was located. I wasn't there very long when I was told that the MACV (Major Army Command Vietnam) chaplain's office had ordered me to fly up to their offices in Saigon, ASAP! Little did I know that the head chaplain for all of Vietnam had other plans for me. Chaplain Bell and his deputy Fr. "Red" Ketchersid had decided that I would go to IV Corps headquarters in Cantho as a replacement for the priest who was returning to CONUS (Continental United States). I was perhaps naive and daring enough to argue that I had been assured by the Chief of Chaplains in Washington that my assignment was to the Fifth Special Forces. I even threatened to resign my commission. I lost the fight but was later to win the battle. I reported to IV Corps headquarters in Cantho and got my "baptism by fire" on the very first night of my arrival. An American civilian who lived in the compound and worked for Catholic Charities was giving me a tour of the city when we were suddenly stopped by a Vietnamese guard and advised us to return to our compound. Something was up! That very first evening as I lay asleep in my tiny room, I was awakened by loud explosions all over our compound. TET, the annual Vietnamese New Year's celebration, had begun! I got up and put on my gear, then ran out to the soccer field where helicopters were landing and unloading the wounded. Instinctively I began giving the last rites to the wounded and dying. After a sleepless night I spent the next day signing in and getting briefed. A Protestant Chaplain and I would be flying out in helicopters to all the MACV camps on the Delta. On my first flight to one of the MACV camps that I had heard a knocking noise on my side of the helicopter and wondered whether he was aware of it. He just laughed and remarked: "Chaplain, that knocking sound came from shots being fired at us." I quickly learned to accustom myself to different sounds.

Soon I was transferred to an Aviation unit in Vinh Long where I spent even more hours in the "Huey" (helicopter). My "hooch" (living quarters) was just behind my small chapel which often received mortar rounds. I quickly scrounged a piece of PSP (a metal strip used for the airstrips), placed it under my mattress and on the cot. Whenever there was an incoming mortar sound, I would crawl under that cot, just to be on the safe side.

The day finally arrived when I received orders to report to the 5th SFG, and once again wear my Green Beret. I was greeted by the Group Commander, a Colonel Ladd, and Chaplain LTC Dick Combs. Both had been stationed on Okinawa at the same time I was there also, so I felt right at home.

The Air Force had a small unit there with air field and aircraft to support our operations, and a very nice chapel.

I immediately knew what my mission would be and so every time I visited a team I would repeat three words to myself, words I used to see at railroad crossings: STOP, LOOK, LISTEN. *Stop*, for me meant that I must always visit any site or location where there were Green Berets. *Look*, was to remind me to find the soldier, whether in his hooch, the team house (bar), or lookout post. *Listen;* make the soldier feel comfortable enough to talk about his loved ones back home, his personal problems etc. Not to shock the reader, but the Team House (club) was where I always held my religious services. On every wall of the bar were the centerfolds of Playboy issues. But this was the only place big enough for my Masses, and I knew that the Good Lord didn't mind it one bit. There were four of us Chaplains, two Protestant and two Catholic, one for each of the four Corps. We rotated at the end of the month in order to cover the over one hundred A sites in the country. Getting to each site was often difficult, we were known as the "Circuit Riders", and always hitched rides from the pilots supplying the troops. The exception was Christmas and Thanksgiving Day. On Christmas a personal chopper was provided to each of us so that we might provide a religious service to as many sites as possible.

On Thanksgiving Day we distributed full turkey meals to every camp. I have many memories of my first tour. I had just begun working with the Fifth Group when I was quickly told to go up to Da Nang where the camp at the foot of Marble Mountain had been attacked and several of our Green Berets had been killed. As soon as I got there we held a Memorial Service right where the VC had infiltrated. Attendance by Americans and Vietnamese was proof of a true "Brotherhood".

On another occasion a team member came running up to me and said: "Sir, remember my team leader "Hoss", the guy who said he had no use for religion? Well, we were out on a mission walking through tall elephant grass, when two gunships suddenly spotted us and came down ready to fire on us. Ole Hoss suddenly makes the sign of the cross and begins motioning to the attacking choppers. They fly away and he shouts out: "God is alive and doing well!" This man began coming to my services whenever I visited.

On visits to a camp in the Delta a Major O'Leary would always announce that the chaplain was coming and invited his men to attend a service in the team room. Well, on one visit this good major asked me to accompany him after my service and "check" the perimeter. It was dark, and halfway around he suddenly hands me an M-16 and asks me to walk in front of the jeep, as a kind of a "point man". I thought he was joking but he was serious. I later was told that he just wanted to show his men that they had a Green Beret chaplain. Weeks later I held a Memorial Service for him and his sergeant who were killed as they were checking the camp perimeter.

Up North in I Corps just outside Ben Hoa, another officer, LTC Cerrone, asked me to accompany him and two of his officers as he flew around his area of operation. We were only about five or ten minutes from base when suddenly our helicopter developed engine trouble and we "gyrated" down into a rice paddy and VC territory. I worried a bit when the pilot radioed back to base asking for help, and worried even more when the good Colonel hands me his 45 pistol. I tell him that chaplains are not allowed to carry weapons. He just stares at me and tells me that if I want to live I had better be prepared to use that pistol. After what seemed an eternity another chopper finally arrived. I thanked the Good Lord.

Years later, I would meet Colonel Cerrone's son who, after his ordination as a Catholic priest, became an Army chaplain.

Martha Raye, the famed comedienne from Hollywood would visit Special Forces every Christmastime and entertain the troops at 'A' sites. She had no fear whatsoever and she was the darling of the men. She could "walk the walk and talk the talk" of the men. We would cross paths on many of our visits. When she saw that I would usually carry a bagful of airborne religious medals she would take them from me and distribute them herself. I didn't mind because I knew that the men would treasure these medals coming from her rather than from me. Several years later

I visited "Maggie" at her home in Bel Aire. I was visiting my mother in San Diego so I called "Maggie", just to say hello. Maggie never took "no" for an answer, so I drove up one evening to pay a short visit. I was so surprised at her "team room". On every wall were plaques and certificates she had received from troops that she visited in Vietnam. After an evening of recollecting and drinking (she loved her scotch) I drove back to San Diego . . . (Very carefully!).

I sometimes would meet French Catholic missionaries still working in Vietnam and would try helping them in their missions. Orphanages were plentiful and the Vietnamese nuns running them often requested help, so we would bring them whatever we could scrounge (we were good at this) for them. I had never witnessed the humanitarian tasks that the men would undertake with the suffering civilians. They would build classrooms, dig wells, provide medical care, and build bridges. No task was too great for them.

82nd AIRBORNE DIVISION
FORT BRAGG, NORTH CAROLINA
1969-1970

Arriving at Ft. Bragg for the second time I signed in at headquarters and was further assigned to the 325th Infantry Brigade. I was given additional coverage of the OCS (Officer Candidate School) and the Rangers. It seemed that the brigade was always on alert so all of us, chaplains and chaplain assistants, kept all our gear in my office at Central Chapel. When we were alerted at any hour of the day or night I would just be prepared, with my Chaplain Team, board the buses which would transport us to Pope Air Force Base, sit on the tarmac all "chuted up" and wait. And wait we did so many times. But, that's why the "All American" 82nd Airborne was always ready! One of my chaplains was Fr. Edwin O'Brien, who went on to become the archbishop for the Catholic Military Archdiocese in Washington DC and is now a Cardinal of the Church.

During this tour I was able to sign up for the Jumpmaster Course offered here. I now had the required number of required jumps and I desperately wanted those "master-blaster wings".

Flying instructions were offered by a civilian group at Fort Bragg so I signed up for flying instructions, took solo flights but never got my license because of suddenly getting orders for my second tour to the Fifth

Special Forces Group. I honestly had enjoyed my assignment to the 82nd Airborne, however, I felt that I needed to return to the Green Berets.

RETURN TO SPECIAL FORCES
VIETNAM
1968-1970

This time I flew directly to Tan San Nhut Airport in Saigon, and this time MACV Chaplain's Office did not attempt to rescind my orders. I immediately got on a C-130, headed for Nha Trang where I met Colonel Mike Healy, the Group Commander. He was a flamboyant, hard charging leader who seemed to know just about anyone in Vietnam. He often would meet with senior Vietnamese officials throughout South Vietnam. Whenever he wanted to meet with one of the bishops he would have me flown in an Air America plane, bring the clergyman into our compound and then escort the bishop back to his location. I found this all so intriguing.

Upon his retirement Colonel "Iron Mike" Healy went back to his home in Chicago and went to work for the Police Department.

Our mission as chaplains remained basically the same as in my first tour. Almost daily we would "hitch" a helicopter ride to the A sites, bringing mail, some supplies, good cheer and a religious service. We continued with our civic action in and around our headquarters. I was amazed at the ability of my men in scrounging food, clothing, medicines, and building materials for orphanages and small Montagnard villages.

About half way through my tour we were notified that Fifth Special Forces Group would be returning to CONUS. Suddenly, those of us who still had time on our tour, began to wonder and ask what would become of us. Would we be transferred to another unit?

We, who were remaining, would become "TSH" (training support headquarters) whose special mission would be to continue with the training of Montagnard recruits at some of our remaining sites. We would be wearing the standard Army baseball cap instead of the Green Beret; however, we would still be recognized as Special Forces people.

The day arrived when the men of the Fifth Special Forces Group, the men of the "Green Beret", marched proudly in formation toward the aircraft that would take them and the colors back to Fort Bragg. I was asked to give the final benediction and all I could think of at the end of my prayer were the words of St. Paul: "You have fought the good fight, you have won the race".

It was difficult, emotionally, to see this 5th Group leave; but it was time. Conventional troops were coming in; the type of war in which America had been involved had changed. We members of Training Support Headquarters must continue to prepare the Montagnards and some "Nungs" to become soldiers.

Our headquarters area was drastically reduced in size. We lost our chapel, so I had to build one in another location. Of all places, I had our Filipino civilian workers change what was formerly a small "club" into a very small but adequate chapel. This is where I would say Mass, and perform my first Vietnamese / American wedding. One of our sergeants had lived here long enough for him to begin living with a pretty Vietnamese secretary and had two beautiful Eurasian children. Both were Catholic and wanted their marriage blessed and their children baptized, so, after a few instructions I arranged for a special Mass and baptism in that little chapel followed by a great celebration with Americans and Vietnamese enjoying the occasion.

Time was passing all too quickly for me and I began thinking about my next assignment.

The 10th Special Forces Group in Germany seemed like the best place for me. I wanted to get back to "SF"; I wanted to wear that Green Beret again. After requesting an inter-theatre transfer I didn't have to wait too long before receiving my orders to the 10th SFG.

TENTH SPECIAL FORCES GROUP
BAD TOELZ, GERMANY
1970-1974

After a thirty-day leave with family, I got a flight from Chicago to Frankfurt International Airport and then to Munich, where I was picked up and driven to Bad Toelz. This long trip gave me jet lag which lasted for several days. For days I would be half asleep during the day and wide awake at night.

Flint Kaserne, former garrison for a special Nazi unit, was located in southern Bavaria just outside the quaint town of Bad Toelz. It was surrounded by majestic mountains which were beautifully covered with green forests in the summer and snow-capped in the winter. The town was picture perfect. The small grocery stores, the bakeries, the river running through the middle of the city. I loved spending free time visiting the shops.

The building in the Kazerne contained the offices, classrooms, clinic, Post Exchange, and the USAREUR (US Army Europe) NCO academy. It surrounded a huge quadrangle on all four sides. Outside the Kaserne was a small airfield run by an Air Force captain, and just in front of the main entrance was our small but beautiful chapel. Across the street from the Kaserne was a grade school as well as additional family housing.

As soon as I signed in I reported to the Group commander, Colonel Ludwig Faistenhammer, a veteran of the Vietnam conflict when I was also there. He was a true Green Beret, friendly but firm. Even though he and his wife were faithful Catholics, always attending my Sunday Mass, he was all business when on duty. Once a week he would have an inspection in the large quadrangle and woe be to you if you didn't have a decent haircut, well ironed uniform, and spit-shined boots. It was like being back at Jump School. He would punish us with a "fine", that is, a donation to our chapel or to a charitable organization of one's choice. When he inspected my chapel he would begin with the chapel proper and then our offices. With white gloves he would glide his hands over, under and behind every desk and closet. I can still hear him telling me: "Chaplain, it's the little things that count."

The community from the NCO Academy side and the Special Forces was extremely close. Protestant and Catholic Services were well attended. Our teenagers met weekly as one Youth Group. Our Sergeant Major Pioletti and his family became close friends. One of his daughters became an officer in the Air Force years later and had kept in contact with me. His son, John, joined the Marines.

I recall the Chapel community getting together and organizing a tour to the Holy Land. I was supportive of their plans but wasn't interested in going. It took one of the officer's wives, who happened to be Jewish, to convince me that it was my "duty" to accompany them. To this day I think of the young lady who "lured" me into accompanying them for this trip turned out to be one of the greatest tours I have ever taken: the

Holy Land. Now, whenever I read one of the gospels, I imagine myself present wherever Jesus traveled. I also had the opportunity to go to Oberamergau where "The Passion Play" was presented every ten years; I was even able to understand with my limited knowledge of German.

There was a Retreat Center in Bertchesgaden located in the Alps which was available for members of the Armed Forces. Once a year all Catholic Chaplains stationed in Europe were invited for a week of spiritual renewal involving prayer and conferences.

Training for the 10th Group was consistent. Our HALO and SCUBA teams often met and trained with soldiers of other nations. Whenever possible I would travel with some and spend just a few days with them. We would parachute on to military bases in Germany, France, Denmark, Italy and Spain.

I accompanied one of our teams to Spain whose mission was to train the Spanish Navy water-airborne tactics. We were flown from Munich to Madrid and then to the Navy Base near Cartagena a beautiful city on the East Coast of Spain. I looked forward to time on a beautiful beach. However, one of our young Lieutenants went and volunteered me for a job. He told me that his Spanish sailor friends had asked whether we had a Catholic Chaplain who might be SCUBA qualified and would bless and carry a statue of the Virgin Mary, then dive into an underwater cave and place the statue on a pedestal they had placed in that cave. I could have choked my Lieutenant friend. I hadn't done any SCUBA diving since Okinawa, and I still wondered about sharks. So, on a nice sunny afternoon four of us dove down into the cave and made the Spanish sailors happy. Eventually, I did get some time on the beach.

Returning to Germany we continued with training. Lake Chiemse, a recreational location about an hour's drive from Bad Toelz, had a hotel, gift shops and boating facilities for the Americans. I had accompanied some of our troops to a make a "water jump" on the beautiful lake. Dressed in a "wet suit" and in our parachute we climbed aboard helicopters that would drop us over the lake. Once landing on the Lake we would release ourselves from the chute and then get picked up by rubber boats. When my turn came to jump, I jumped! But when I noticed that all those on the "stick" I had jumped with were already back on shore and I was still on a level with the helicopters dropping other troops, I began to worry . . . . and pray! I had been caught up into what I think they called an air-pocket, and I was not descending. When the men below me began shouting for me to pull a riser in order to "deflate" the chute I truly worried . . . and prayed. I pulled on my risers to partially deflate my canopy, and then began to descend. Again my men got a big kick out of the incident. "Your Boss probably wanted to keep you", they joked.

Cross-country snow-shoeing was another exercise. With full winter clothing and full rucksack we would march out into the neighboring mountains, get into the snow rackets and climb up and down those snow-covered mountains until I thought I would die. Even the tent that I was to sleep in for the night and those horrible MRIs were most welcome.

One pleasant TDY was to Munich, Germany. The Munich Olympics were held in this beautiful city and naturally many of our Americans were participating. When a Senior Chaplain in Munich asked if I would come up for a few days, stay at the Village for our Americans and just be available for all of them, I certainly volunteered. Some months before I had been up to the city for the "Oktoberfest"; so I did have some good times.

After Colonel Faistenhammer left there was a commander whose name I won't mention, but who was a disappointment. An incident occurred which made me realize how important and necessary it was for a chaplain to stand up for what is right.

A young soldier and his wife came to me one day accusing one of the senior NCO's of sexual harassment with some of the wives in the battalion. They gave me sufficient proof and begged for me to do something. When I approached the senior sergeant's Commander and the Group Commander I was disappointed when they got on the defensive. The lieutenant colonel remarked, "Aw, come on, Chappy, a man's gotta have a little fun". I blurted out: "Sir, if you don't do anything I will go to higher head-quarters." Only then was this sergeant transferred. Later on even his wife would confirm the accusations.

I would continue with my ministry there until I heard about an offer I just could not refuse. The USAEURER Chaplain who was in charge of all Army Chaplains in Europe announced that the Army was offering a TDY (temporary duty) position for any Army priest interested in attending a three month Theology Renewal Course in Rome. I had just a few months left with the 5th Group so I immediately applied and I was so surprised when I received word that I was selected.

One of my best priest friends had also made the request and when he got word that I had been chosen he called me up and remarked, "Mike, I can't believe this. First, you beat me to the Special Forces slot and now again to that course in Rome". "Nick," I said, "I just prayed a little harder". This priest had been an NYC policeman, a vocation director, a Special Forces Chaplain and won two Silver Stars for heroism in Vietnam.

TEMPORARY DUTY TO
ROME, ITALY
1974

I laugh heartily now when I recall my drive from my place in Bad Toelz, Germany. The beautiful mountains with the long tunnels, the quaint villages along the "Autostrada" were a sight to behold and enjoy. As I was nearing the outskirts of the Eternal City, I couldn't help but notice people, mostly young ladies, milling around small fire-places (it was a very chilly evening). I imagined that these poor people were just warming themselves until the buses came. Upon arriving at the "Casa Maria", where I was to reside, and sitting around with some of the faculty members I mentioned this observation to them and they just laughed. Those young ladies, they told me, belonged to the oldest profession known to man. Thank God I didn't offer any of them a lift into town.

Rome is an enormously large, congested city with autos, buses, trams, and Vespas moving every which way. Pockmarked with Roman ruins, catacombs, churches and shops, it never seems to stop.

Our school, called the "Casa Maria" was located in the very heart of the tourist attractions. The buildings were completely enclosed and just a block away from the "Trevi Fountain". I often hummed the popular song: "Three Coins in a Fountain".

After our classes many of us would get together and either go out for a good Italian dinner or just have a "gelato" or some strong Italian coffee before retiring. Our course was tailored to those of us who had been ordained ten years or more and brought us up-to-date on the latest changes in the Church.

While in Rome I had an old friend who came to visit and, since I had my car we were able to drive out into the countryside and even to Castel Gondolfo where the Pope was living during those hot summers in Rome. Even at his summer residence Pope John Paul II had crowds waiting for his blessing from a balcony.

One of our classes was Church History. We visited so many Churches and the catacombs. We were given a week's break so I chose to travel to Prague and Budapest. I must say that I am forever grateful for the Army to have given me the opportunity to learn more about my faith and how to practice it.

The highlight of our stay in Rome was a visit to the Vatican and assisting in a Mass by the Holy Father. The day I was to drive back to Germany, I was able to say a private Mass at one of the side altars in St. Peter's. Just as I began my Mass a young American couple came up to me, asked if I was American, and whether they could attend my Mass. It made me proud to have this couple, from my country, assist in my final celebration of the Eucharist in Rome.

COMMAND & GENERAL STAFF COLLEGE
FORT LEAVENWORTH, KANSAS
1978-1979

When I wrote and told my brothers in Indiana that I was being sent to Fort Leavenworth they worried that I had gotten into serious trouble. The Command and General Staff College is actually situated next to the Federal prison. It sits next to the city of Leavenworth and just as old. In my class there were a total of nine-hundred-and-seventy officers from the Army, Navy, and Marines. There were also fifty officers from other allied forces. We were broken up into twenty-two sections.

The course offered here was geared especially for line officers who were making the Army their career and with the potential of quick promotions. I did think of making the Army a career but certainly not for any promotions. During my time there was a limit to one's tenure in Special Forces so I knew that my time was about up. Command and General Staff College was strictly an academic institution involving a lot of research work. My classmates were the excellent officers and I learned much from them. Retired General Eric Shinseki, now secretary to the VA was a classmate and a friend.

Salina, Kansas was my place of birth, and though I remembered little of that town, and because it was not far from Leavenworth, I decided to one day drive over and later tell my mother I had visited the place where she got married and where I was born.

As I drove through the main street I saw tractor trailers loaded with bales of hay. I now recognized the wisdom of my father in moving us to Indiana. He was no farmer and preferred the steel mills of Northern Indiana to the wheat fields of Kansas.

FIRST INFANTRY DIVISION
GOEPPINGEN, GERMANY
1979

Upon graduation I received orders assigning me as Division Chaplain to the First Infantry Division. I must admit that I was excited about the move because I now had the opportunity to learn about what my classmates would call the "real Army".

Located in Goeppingen, the "Big Red One" headquarters was heavily involved in maneuvers in Graffenwoehr and Wildflichen. Its Infantry and Armor battalions were almost always traveling up and down the Autobahns come rain, shine, or snow. My officers in charge were very supportive of our chapel program and caring for the families.

One of my sergeants helped me build a "Chapmobile". Since my mode of transportation was an Army pick-up truck in which we carried everything from our tent to MREs, to a huge Coffee container we called "The silver bullet" to my Mass kit, I just didn't see a need to suffer any more than necessary. With the help of a handy NCO we got a discarded VW van, cut off the top part and welded it on to the pick-up, put paneling in the interior, built two small benches which would serve as bunk beds and supply boxes, installed a battery-powered heater and we had a "mobile home". I recall the Germans staring at what looked like a camouflaged hearse driving through their small towns. But, it served the purpose. The tail gate I used as my altar for the services I held out in the field.

The Protestant chaplain and myself had our chaplain assistants always accompany us, something that was not possible with Special Forces, since transportation to outlying teams was always a problem just for the chaplain.

After about a year with the 1st Infantry, I was promoted and transferred to Seventh Army Headquarters as the Deputy Corps Chaplain. My mission now was to travel throughout the Corps visiting, inspecting and supporting all of our chaplains. I missed being with the young troops. While in Stuttgart I celebrated my 25th Anniversary as a priest so the Commander arranged a surprise banquet and granted me a 30 day leave to celebrate with my family and friends.

I returned and completed my tour until orders came for me to return to Ft. Benning, Georgia as Deputy Chaplain.

RETURN TO
FORT BENNING, GEORGIA
1982

The Post Chaplain, Col. Andrews, was a very good friend of mine and, as his Deputy, allowed me get involved in almost any type of ministry I chose. Of course, I volunteered to help the Airborne Chaplains, of course I would help the Special Forces unit who had no chaplain, and of course I would visit the Ranger students training in Dahlonica in Georgia and Camp Eglin in Florida. There was now a shortage of Catholic Chaplains at Fort Bragg but somehow we were able to cover most of the units on Post. Every Sunday evening, after our Masses we would get together for dinner at one of the restaurants in town.

WAR COLLEGE
CARLISLE, PENNSYLVANIA
1986-1987

In 1986 I was surprised at being selected for the Army's War College in Carlisle, Pennsylvania. Only three chaplains from the Chaplain's Corps were chosen so we were a minority among several hundred officers from all branches of the service, civilians such as CIA and government personnel and officers from thirty other allied countries. Subjects such as National Policy and Strategy, Regional Appraisal of Foreign Countries, were given in the classrooms and talks by diplomats, Generals, and other important government officials were presented in the well known "Bliss Hall" (called by the students as "Sleepy Hall"). Every student had to write a thesis for publication. I chose: "Confidentiality of the Chaplain". A very good friend and chaplain classmate in this course was Chaplain Matt Zimmerman. He was a big help to me in understanding the make-up of the regular Army. He was later to become a Major General and Chief of Chaplains.

Many of our classes consisted of visiting Congress while in Session at our Nation's Capitol, memorable tour of Gettysburg and the battlefields during our civil war.

Upon completion of our course we all received our orders. I was to go to Panama, as the USARSO (Army South) Chaplain.

FORT CLAYTON, PANAMA
1987

As I moved up in rank I thought I would be stuck behind a desk, but I soon realized that everything depended on my own decisions. The mission of our Command was to oversee, support, and establish good relations with our Latin American neighbors.

SOUTHCOM (Southern Command) was the overall headquarters, composed of Officers of all branches of the service and other government employees. My responsibility would be to provide ministry to all, which meant that again I would be connected to the Infantry, Airborne, logistics units on Fort Clayton and, unofficially at least, to the Eighth Special Forces Group stationed on the opposite side of the Panama Canal. "God is good", I would tell myself.

My quarters (complete house with two bedrooms) was on Colonels' Row surrounded by mango trees, golf course, ball fields and almost any other recreational facility for soldiers and their dependents. I called it "Little America" because it had everything a small city would have back in the USA. There was the American Hospital "Gorgas" not far from Clayton. During Senator John McCain's campaign I learned he had been born at this hospital.

BG Bernard Loefke was our commanding general and quite the man. We used to call him the "Bald Eagle" because, even though relatively young, he was bald, but handsome. General Loefke and I became good friends, even though he was always challenging me in PT. Every morning he made sure I was standing in formation and ready for our four mile run or his popular "King of the Hill" exercise. "C'mon, Chaplain," he would say, "Let's see what you can do." Now he knew I was the oldest man in the group, but I believe he did this to challenge the rest of the soldiers, at my expense.

Outside of PT he would always treat me with respect and, since I spoke Spanish, as he did, would have me accompany him on his visits in-country as well as countries like Peru, Venezuela, Columbia, Belize, and Guatemala.

During my tour in Panama I considered myself fortunate for having hard working chaplains and chaplain assistants. Occasionally chaplains from the Air Force and the Navy would get together and help one another when needed.

One priest friend, Chaplain Paul Freemesser, and I were able to rent a small island right in the Panama Canal. It was about the size of two basketball courts, with a small "Bahio" (hut), with a small dock for our boat, and a concrete floor and a place for grilling.

Once a month we invited other chaplains to come to "Padre Island" and spend the day, swimming, relaxing, grilling, and having a cool beer. Fr. Paul and I ordered a jet-ski and just enjoyed racing up and down the canal. He was quite good at it but I can't count the number of times I would fall off. The good times were not to last.

The end of my tour had finished, and I had orders for Ft. Devens, Massachusetts. My household goods had just been stored in a Conex and prepared for shipment. I had borrowed an Army field cot to sleep on and was sound asleep when all of a sudden I was awakened by gunfire just outside my front window. I got up and saw an armored vehicle firing into the jungle across the road. JUST CAUSE had begun. I certainly was agitated at not having been informed about the invasion by our troops. None of the Chaplains' section was prepared. I quickly dressed and ran to our Main Post Chapel.

I called the hospital to contact the Protestant and Catholic Chaplains assigned there and was told that they were not allowed to leave their living quarters. Agitated even more so I had a Chaplain Assistant drive me in our Humvee to the hospital which was located about five miles outside Fort Clayton. I kept silently praying "Hail Mary's" as we raced down the streets while getting fired at from all sides.

Arriving safely at the hospital the very first dying soldier I anointed was a very young man whom I had met just a few days previously; a blond handsome soldier. He had jumped onto an exploding grenade in order to save his buddies. His body now was charred from head to toe. I continued praying and anointing the wounded and the dead until the following morning when the two hospital chaplains were finally allowed to come to their positions.

Upon my return to Ft. Clayton I was finally briefed and then began preparing for the Rangers and the 82nd Airborne who had arrived for "Just Cause". We turned our Church Hall into a kind of USO where the soldiers could come, relax, call home, or just have something to drink or a sandwich or two.

Our new commander, BG Cisneros had been assigned to USARSO recently. Upon learning that I was leaving, and that my replacement spoke no Spanish, he asked if I would be willing to extend. When I told him that my replacement was already en route, he said that he would ask the chief of chaplains to allow me to extend as his Advisor. Within a few short days I received my new orders. I moved up to headquarters and was given an office adjacent to the General's.

The very first task I was given was to minister to Panama's President, Vice-president and their families, who had been given shelter in Fort Clayton. Then the General asked me to make contact with Bishops McGrath and Brown as well as the Apostolic Nuncio.

I now saw the wisdom in General Cisneros keeping me in Panama, at least temporarily.

I visited the Apostolic Nuncio's home, where Noriega had found asylum and arranged to drive the Archbishop to the POW camp, where so many of Noriega's men were kept.

Most of my duties as Advisor consisted of accompanying General Cisneros whenever he visited local leaders and military, visiting and helping Catholic Charities purchase land tillers for villages, as well as building materials, and working with Archbishop McGrath. When everything was restored and

Noriega imprisoned in the States, my time to depart soon arrived, but instead of going to Fort Devens, Massachusetts I was sent to Fort Sam Houston, Texas.

FIFTH ARMY
SAN ANTONIO, TEXAS
1990-1993

Texas is "big" and so is the city of San Antonio. Many a night some of us would go to the "River Walk", take tours of the Alamo and other tourist sites. Fort Sam Houston is an old historical installation right in the city and reminds me of Flint Kaserne in Germany. The buildings are connected and form a square or quadrangle where deer, peacocks and tame squirrels would roam around freely. The quadrangle also serves as a parade ground for many occasions.

As Fifth Army chaplain I was responsible for overseeing the Reserve and National Guard Chaplains and Chaplain Assistants in all the Western States so I spent most of my time on the road. "Desert Storm" had begun so my office activated a fair number of chaplains who were very quickly shipped to Saudi Arabia.

My Chaplain recruiter, who was Protestant, would always ask me to accompany him whenever he visited the bishop of the dioceses for which we were responsible. To my surprise, Bishops, only after a personal interview, would allow priests to join the Chaplaincy.

I believe it was here in San Antonio where I met the now retired Chief of Chaplains, Father Chess. It took place at spiritual gathering of Army and Air Force priests. I reminded him that some twenty five years earlier he had told me that I wasn't fit for the Air Force Chaplaincy. With a sly smile I thanked him for having made it possible for me to join the "Green Berets".

FORT CARSON, COLORADO
1992-1995

My final assignment was Fort Carson, just south of Colorado Springs and home of the Fourth Infantry. Also located just north of the city was the Air Force Academy, and west of Fort Carson up in a mountain that, at the time, was the highly classified Air Force monitoring Center.

As installation and command chaplain I again was responsible for overseeing the entire religious program on the Post. The division, like any Infantry unit was always on exercises and the chaplains were always out in the field with their men but we almost always managed to do our PT as a team. At my age I was beginning to slow down a bit but my pride made me try to keep up with the "young ones". We Catholic Chaplains were usually older than other officers in rank, because of years of study prior to becoming chaplains; however, we were required to keep up with our peers.

Colorado Springs seemed to me a modern western city but still western. In the center of the city was the well known Olympic Training Center.

My chaplain section had a lodge several miles south of our Post which was continuously used for spiritual retreats, conferences, and social gatherings. In addition we acquired a building in the division area and converted into a recreation center which we called "Interlude" where the young soldiers could come and relax.

One of my highlights was Pope John Paul's visit to Denver during the World Youth Convention. I was able to get some tickets for some of my soldiers.

President Clinton was welcoming the Pope and as they exited the plane and walked toward a sedan one of my Catholic soldiers called out to the Pope in Polish and the Holy Father turns around and approaches the soldier and briefly speaks to him in Polish. The young soldier had migrated to the US and certainly never dreamed he would be seeing his countryman, the Pope, in America.

I was always fortunate in getting the assignments keeping me close to the young men and women in uniform, and this, my last assignment, would afford me the opportunity to hold services for Catholics in the field. The Protestant chaplains were remarkable in getting me transportation, and scheduling the service during breaks. This is where I learned what RIP meant in the military (rank has its privileges).

Only a few times in my career did I encounter commanders with whom I did not see eye to eye. My last incident was with an unnamed Brigadier General who attempted to remove me for insubordination. I had assigned a young black chaplain by the name of Dave Hicks to the main Post chapel. A few of the old retired Protestant men complained to the general who came to me and insisted I make some changes. I actually refused so it wasn't long before the FORSCOM (Forces Command) chaplain flew in from

Atlanta, Georgia. We knew each other personally and I explained that I truly believed this was a racial issue and that the General had been influenced by the "elders" (retired old goats) to get me to change my decision. I warned my chaplain friend that I would go to the local newspaper and make an accusation of racial prejudice. To this day I don't know what took place between Chaplain Peterson and the General, but I remained in my position until my retirement. In fact, as my senior rater, this General gave me a very complimentary OER (officer efficiency report).

I mention this incident at the end of this book to show the reader that it never really pays to become a "yes" person for the sake of advancement, or to merely be liked by one's superior.

I don't believe I have ever been hurt when I have stood up to my Faith or to the morality I was taught in all my years. Chaplain Dave Hicks, the Black Protestant chaplain whom I assigned to the main Protestant Congregation was the best qualified. In fact, he would later be selected as the Chief of Chaplains for the United States Army!

ACKNOWLEDGEMENTS

Theresa Bagg and her daughter Catherine helped me immensely in getting this book ready for publication. Theresa helped with correcting grammar and formatting the text. Catherine, a student at the University of San Francisco, was responsible for designing the cover. We made a great team and I am grateful for their help.